Diary of a Smart Black Kid: Sixth grade

David M. Taylor II

Main character illustrations by the
Kurian Brothers

Additional illustrations by
Uzma Ghauri and David M Taylor II

HOUSE OF DT BOOKS * SKOKIE, ILLINOIS

Publisher's Cataloging-In-Publication Data (Prepared by The Donohue Group, Inc.)

Names: Taylor, David M., II, 1964- author, illustrator. | Kurian, Jacob, 1987- illustrator. | Kurian, Paul, illustrator. | Ghauri, Uzma, illustrator.
Title: Diary of a smart black kid. Sixth grade / by David M. Taylor II ; main character illustrations by the Kurian Brothers ; additional illustrations by Uzma Ghauri and David M. Taylor II.
Other Titles: Sixth grade
Description: 1st edition. | Skokie, Illinois : House of DT Books, 2017. | Interest age level: 010-013. | Summary: "Baron Winters, an eleven year old African-American male, chronicles his year in sixth grade, with all of the associated troubles that come along with being a geeky, smart, black kid."-- Provided by publisher.
Identifiers: ISBN 9780988821699 (softcover) | ISBN 9780988821682 (ebook)
Subjects: LCSH: African American boys--Diaries--Juvenile fiction. | Gifted children--Diaries--Juvenile fiction. | Sixth grade (Education)--Juvenile fiction. | CYAC: African American boys--Diaries--Fiction. | Gifted children--Diaries--Fiction. | Schools--Fiction.
Classification: LCC PZ7.1.T39 Di 2017 (print) | LCC PZ7.1.T39 (ebook) | DDC [Fic]--dc23

Diary of a Smart Black Kid: Sixth Grade
1st edition, Soft Cover – Published in 2017 by
HOUSE OF DT BOOKS, PO Box 693, Skokie, IL 60076-0693. ISBN   978-0-9888216-9-9
Library of Congress Control Number: 2017913452

Printed in the USA 10 9 8 7 6 5 4 3 2 1

For permission or requests, write to the Publisher: HOUSE OF DT BOOKS
PO Box 693
Skokie, IL 60076-2025
info@houseofdtbooks.com
www.HouseofDTBooks.com

DEDICATION

I dedicate this book to every child who ever felt like they didn't fit in.

Which is all of us.

Table of Contents

CHAPTER 1

So I almost got shot today - End of Summer Part 1

AUGUST

Friday

So I almost got shot today. But I'll get to the gun thing in a minute. See, I love summer bike riding in my hometown. It's homey! Also. I might be using cycle therapy (see what I did there?) to casually ignore the fact that it's almost here.

"It" meaning, the test that will change my life.

Well 'almost' actually meaning springtime next year. Still. WOO HOO! Yeah, only geeks count days until tests. So color me count-y. There's something happening in my life even sooner, however. That would be the Blessed Advent of Junior High School. And by 'Blessed Advent' I mean 'yeah I'm scared brainless.' Sixth grade is just a few days away. Sixth grade. *In a few days*. I need to do really well this year in school to even qualify for the test in the spring.

But in the *meantime,* I need to graze in every boy's natural habitat: sweat! According to my mother every time I take a shower I'm wasting water and running up the electric bill. Haven't figured that one out yet. But what I *do* know is that It's August and that means bike riding 'til it's dark. Till dark, I tells ya! Also. Adults and kids have different definitions of 'dark.'

Speaking of my hometown, it's right outside Chicago. Lots of bike paths. Although I prefer riding in the streets. I probably shouldn't tell my parents that I played chicken with a bus one time. Yeah maybe I'll leave that out of our next dinner 'So how was your day?' discussion.

August is a funny month. I'm pretty sure it's named after Augustus. Who was like, the first Roman emperor. And I know that more babies are born in August. My mind's kind of buzzy like that, all funny factoid n' thangs. Maybe that's not one hundred percent true because my big sister Christina (she's eighteen) was born in May and my big brother Zeke (he's twenty-one, SO old) was born in December. But that was with dad's first wife and not my mom so does that make the August thing totally bogue? Anyway. August is still like the last dance with summer, so it has all these really hot days. Maybe so you can like soak up some extra sunshine or heat or something because winter will make you forget all of this.

Then there's Friday, which has to be, like, the best day of the week ever. It's the only day of the week where's there no downside. Like if candy were turned into a day. Because:

-No work the next day

-Allowance money comes

-Cartoons and pancakes all morning

-You can sleep until the sun stops talking

Also. Every single sleepover in the history of people has happened on a Friday night. Then there's pizza, which has to be like, celestial in origin. Greek gods ate ambrosia and nectar. American gods eat pizza. I'm sure there's a god law that says so. Pizza was invented for Fridays. Pizza is the king of food.

So I think that makes Friday like, the king of days. Or it would be if there was a contest for such things. Like Friday would beat up Thursday and take Wednesday's girlfriend and exile Monday. Because who loves Mondays? Nobody, that's who.

Tuesday is clearly like that kid that nobody notices except when they do something crazy. Like for example when it follows a three-day weekend. Then Tuesday feels like Monday part deux and ugh. Three day weekends are always fun though because they're like extra ketchup on a burger. I have noticed that my big brother and sister seem to be able to pack more fun into their weekends than I can. I guess that's part of the benefits of being older. I'm not even fully a teenager and already it seems like being a non-teenager is the coolest thing ever. Except for maybe Minecraft. I can't imagine anything out-cooling that. Hey wait wouldn't it be awesometacular if Friday got in a fight with Minecraft to see which one was cooler? I'm pretty much figuring there is a magical place where all this stuff that kids imagine actually happens, or else why would we be able to imagine it? Well. Anyway. Friday wins all battles and sometimes I wish it could be forty-eight hours long because that would rock like Ben Grimm in a mudslide. Friday is life.

Except for the fact that this particular Friday there was that gun thing with the cop. I was downtown in my second favorite bookstore, Kirst & Dorsten. This cop followed me out of the store. Then he watched me unchain my bike from the rack. Like he didn't believe it was mine. I wanted to get out of there in a hurry so I started moving faster (because what kid likes being stared down by law enforcementicals?) Then he totally pulled his gun on me. I had to drop my bike and my lock, and faceplant myself.

Running down my leg, my sweat shook hands with my pee and said in unison "we're in trouble." I just never pictured dying before my first year of junior high school. Fortunately, after he saw my highly trembly demeanor Officer Not-So-Friendly seemed to no longer think I was a thief.

I think.

So I left. (note to self: put an I.D. tag on your bike when you get home. Oh and change your pants.) Maybe I should get a tattoo on my bike that says "Property of Baron Winters." Because I could never get like, a real tattoo. My mother would look at me like I grew a second face. Then she'd break the one I have.

So I pretty much decided I wasn't gonna let Captain Overanxious back there suck the joy out of my day. Even though he almost Rodney King'd me. Yeah, I watched those videos. History Maaaaan! Plus if I qualify to take that test at all, nothing's gonna stop me from doing well on it. That's just not gonna happen. But I've got a whole school year to get through before I'm there. And I'm gonna live in Comic Book World until then. Oh um along with studying of course. Hashtag not a slacker. #NotaSlacker

I had gone into Kirst & Dorsten because I didn't have time to ride all the way across town to the Comic Shop. Sometimes K & D has some comic books. Although lately, my allowance was on life support after a trip to buy some comics. Comics are like, five dollars per book. I love love LOVE the Comic Shop tho. They have everything. Comic books, RPGS, action figures

(They. Are. Not. Dolls.), game nights, DVDs, posters. I could just live there. I would if I could afford it. Jeezum Lord a'Mercy I could just see the drama if I asked my dad for more allowance money. I wouldn't recommend *that* to my worst enemy.

Well actually, I would because I can't stand that evil Derek Kilroy. But. Anyway. I haven't figured out yet why the stuff you hate the most takes up so much brain space. But then again I guess the stuff you love the most does too. Life's kind of funny that way but when I grow up, I'm gonna invent some kind of brain filter memory device.

Like...like...totally awesome Forgetto Glasses!

TOTALLY AWESOME

FORGETTO GLASSES™

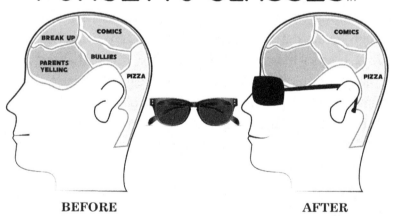

BEFORE   AFTER

Holy mother of haggis they will be the best-selling thing ever. Know why? Because what people wouldn't give to be able to have selective memory. Know how I know that? Because all parents in the League of Adultage have selective memory. They can't seem to remember all the stuff you've done right when they're yelling at you. Just the things you do wrong. I'd like to perfect that and then flip the switch so I could only remember the good things.

Then again, what would happen if you didn't know how to classify a memory? Yikes, I sense a bug in the software. Oh well, I'd figure out a way to classify memories for targeted removal. Because I totally could.

If I wasn't already such a genius I would invent patented Genius Pills™ and turn myself into a genius.

Eeeyup I have solved all problems.

CHAPTER 2

My house is a pulpit. Apparently.

Saturday

My parents are not together. Officially. Or technically. Or something. Anyways I live with my mom in the 'burbs and my dad has his own apartment. We live in a house on the north side and since Zeke has moved out I have a room all to myself. SCORE! Isn't that what big brothers are for tho? To give little brothers all their stuff? I could be wrong but I'm not asking for a recount on that one. I see my dad on third weekends and whenever he comes over here, on his totally random drive-by parenting visits. He comes over on most holidays and they pretend like we're still together as a family. Sometimes he even sleeps over here. Um, their 'arrangement' may be a source of cornfusement for me but don't quote me on that. So if I understand it correctly they're not really able to make their marriage work, so their strategy? Is to lecture *me* to death. Okay then.

My parents always say things to me like, "Wait 'til you get grown! You'll see!" I'm not quite sure what such soliloquies are designed to do. Am I supposed to fear adulthood? Or run towards it? Then they say things like "You're living your best days now!!" They never say *that* one quietly, either. I keep wondering to myself...do they think I have a choice? I mean, as to how long I get to stay a child? That makes no sense to me. And if these are my best days...yeesh. It's really funny listening to adults talk because it's quite obvious to me that they think that we should think like *they* do. I'm in sixth grade. I can't look at life the same way my dad does. How could I? But somehow that seems to be an endless source of delight for them, telling me how much I don't know. My response to that is, as opposed to what? Are there any kids in SIXTH. GRADE. who have life all figured out yet? If such a kid exists I'd sure like to meet him.

Then again he'd probably be so pretentious and arrogant until I couldn't stay in the same room with him. Like all the mega-brainiacs at school. Geez. Let a person win a spelling bee in fifth grade and all of a sudden they're Ultra Lord High Commander over the rest of their class.

All this thinking has made me thirsty. But I know what mom will say. She says it every time I walk into the kitchen looking for something to drink. "Too much sugar for you, young man." Errrr...maybe if you don't want me to like those drinks you shouldn't buy them for me? Everybody knows that sugar is like, drugs for kids. YIKES, I would never say that to her, though. Is that being a smart mouth when I say that? I think so. Is honesty illegal for kids? I think that's it. Maybe I should create some laws to help myself keep it all straight.

<u>Baron's Law:</u>

Kids can't speak the truth out loud.

That's a teeth saver right there! But back to my liquid glucose dilemma. I mean I could just go over to Z's house and drink them anyway but still. Yeah, so that's it. I just have to accept it. Being a kid is about being silent and pretending that you're dumber than you are.

Adults seem to really like that.

CHAPTER 3

The beach is a strange place - End of Summer Part 2

Sunday

Is it just me, or do people not know how to dress for their height and weight? I mean, beaches are like a flab convention for people that wish they were cute down here. (See, that's another thing that if I said it out loud I'd get slapped in the mouth by some nearby negro adult. So I just thought it real loud, but wow.) So we (me and mom and Christina) drove down to the beach Sunday after church. It was fun packing for the trip that morning, but hard to keep my mind off of it during service. It was the best kind of warm day, where you can feel the sun on your skin but it's not scorching. Beaches in Chicago are always awesome. And crowded. So we had to walk further than usual because we parked in a new spot. There was like, a really gentle breeze blowing. The beach is another forever place for me. After we get there, I never want to leave. Except for that doggie doo on my shoe thing.

Sometimes people tell me that I'm mean because I'm mostly clear about how I feel about things. Uh, mostly. Then again I am just a kid and this is the last time in my life I get to be this honest. Ohhhhh, I've seen the way adults lie about every single thing in their lives and then demand that us kids tell them the truth. It's not pretty.

Oh look there's Devin Greene, with her little girl dog. Everybody brings their dog to Le Beach. But no one cleans up after Lil' Spike. Or Muffin. Or what *do* people actually name their dogs these days?

I had on my favorite swim trunks, the dark black ones (because *obviously,* they're like Batman's) and I just loved the feeling of the sand in my toes and the smell of the water. Me and Chen Ziang (that's "Z," my best friend) played Frisbee football for like, I dunno three hours or something. Then we had lap races down to the first buoy and back. We tied, as usual.

But coming out of the water, it's like being wet is a sand magnet. WELP that's no fun when you get back in the car. My life is shenanigans.

Also. Why does mom seem to blow a gasket if I use the wrong towel? "Don't you use mah GOOD towels for the beach Baron Winters!" Ummm…okay. Don't all towels do the same thing? No seriously am I missing something? Chen's mom is the same way except with a little less volume. Maybe it's the sand, but does that really hurt a towel? Also. My question has always been, if you're so clean when you get out of the shower, how do towels ever get dirty? See my point here? I dunno, being a genius is hard work because there are so many questions. That's why I like Chen tho, he seems like really calm all the time.

It's great when we hang out. He knows comics better than I do and plays just about every video game that I like. His dad travels a lot for his job so he doesn't seem to get to see him much. That's kind of a bummer. His dad gets a kick out of us being geeks tho, he loves to give Chen money for books. He offered to come to a movie with us one time, but we were like…thanks but no. Parental presence leads to embarrassment. Embarrassment leads to suffering. And suffering leads to the Crackhead Side of The Force.

I think my fave hero is Batman. Mainly because he makes his own decisions and doesn't ask anybody for permission. The other heroes like, seem to worry what people think about them. Not Batman tho, he *wants* you to be scared of him. I think also that I need to start making my own superheroes. I don't see why not. I need to make a hero that is super-fast and can turn invisible and won't get diabetes. Yeah, I'm gonna have to look up 'diabetes' but mom says dad has it and it's bad. So my hero would be able to be undetectable and uninflictable. Now that I think about it, that would be an awfully convenient power set for a sixth grader. I mean, I could pass all my Phys Ed classes with ease, and I could spy on all the bullies in school to be sure I avoided them. Downside? Yeah, I could no longer really claim sick days, could I? Oh well. Maybe I'll draw this guy sooner rather than later.

CHAPTER 4

Puberty. Is there an opt-out button?

Monday, Labor Day

So, Monday morning on Labor Day, feeling all holidayish, I jumped out of bed and walked over to my mirror. And there my not-a-fifth-grader-anymore body was staring back at me. (Yeah I should've brushed my teeth but thankfully mirrors don't have a smell reflection.) I'm wondering if I can signal 'pass' and just bypass puberty altogether. Like enter a life cheat code and just go straight to adulthood. I'm pretty sure puberty is starting. Maybe. How am I supposed to tell? Wait if I can't tell that means it's not starting, right? The only thing I've noticed is that when I get embarrassed my face burns like I poured acid on it.

It's not weird to be jealous of my pet fish Tropey, is it? I mean fish are pretty much who they are all the time. And they just swim and eat. I guess laying eggs is a part of their lives but they never seem to have to get zits to do that. It's like nature saved all the meanest puberty tricks for humans. I could be wrong. I love Tropey tho, he's the coolest goldfish ever. I have so many comics on my floor I dream that Tropey jumps out of his bowl and reads them when I'm asleep. Like, he can't let humans know he can do that so he has to wait until I'm asleep or gone. Yeah, I might be weird.

Also. Is there a puberty psychiatrist, someone that I can talk to about my, um, changes? Or lack thereof? Is that normal? Sometimes I look at my little cousin Randy and remember how much fun it is just to be six years old. I've also noticed that bullies always go through puberty the earliest. It's like life has this plan to be sure that the idiots of this world get well stocked with biceps and facial hair before anyone else.

Nature's Law:

Jerks get muscles first.

Baron's Law:

Jerks seek out smart kids to destroy.

This is why I wish nature had Presidential elections like our country does. So I could vote out whoever passed the 'There MUST be Bullies' law.

Know who I'm not looking forward to seeing? Derek Kilroy. There's a future felon for ya. Every day of fifth grade, he made a beeline for me just to torment me. Here's the thing...I can't even figure out what I did. It's like he took one look at me and decided that beating my life into the ground was his Righteous

Call from On High (cue angel sound *aahhhh*). I might have to ask God about that one day- if it's okay to hate people that hate you. Kilroy the Krazed even has like, a whole Bully Squad that he grunts around with. At least he did last year. Barry Hunt and Jackie Milo round out his Unholy Trinity. Good luck getting adults to listen. I've got a better chance of being struck by a jumbo turd from a flying cow.

This is why every little boy's room doubles as a fortress. It's a Bully free zone and a place to plan. Hide. Read comics. All that stuff. I don't know why the female type parents don't get that. Yet another thing I can't figure out. My big brother Zeke (or Ezekiel on holidays) told me that they didn't really address bullying when he was my age. He just kind of dealt with it and moved on. Well they've given us all kinds of school assemblies and sensitivity training and classroom exercises to deal with this bullying thing. But when one of us actually wants to talk to a school adult? It's like we've got the Stank Breath from Jupiter. I overheard mom one time saying that it was because of lawsuits. Like, if the school actually gets involved they're going to get sued. Umm, then that is what we call the No Win Scenario. Like when you're up against a Boss character at the end of a level two fighting round and no matter what you do, you can't defeat them. Even with an ultra-mega combo super punch at full strength. Which is majorly bogue. That's a big purple ball of frustration if I've ever seen one. Maybe that's another law I need to write down.

Baron's Law:

Adults want to talk at *you. Not* with *you.*

Yeah at the rate I'm writing these life laws I'mma give Moses a run for his money on that whole Ten Commandments thing.

So I looked in my mirror and realized this was it. My last day of summer. And being a fifth grader. Tomorrow I take the plunge into junior high school. My last Labor Day as that version of me. I don't know who started Labor Day, but it's the only Monday that has fans. Because it's the end of the last three-day weekend of summer. And Labor Day is Latin for "all the food you ate on the Fourth of July plus rib tips." That's a beautiful thing. So I read some more comics and then went to the kitchen to get another gut-busting plate of food. That was pretty much a winning plan. And I will take whatever wins I can get!

Also. When you're a kid, there's not a lot of options for being choosy. That whole can't work, can't drive, can't vote thing.

CHAPTER 5

Math was invented by the devil.

SEPTEMBER

Tuesday

First day of junior high school. It's a new level of eerie. Hope I brushed my teeth enough. Mom gave me a ride because it was the first day, but tomorrow? It's the bus for me. She dropped me off and I asked her to please not kiss me because MOM. But she did anyway. So I had to wipe that off with a quickness.

I walked into school. And immediately had the feeling. You know. *That* feeling. The one where everybody's checking you out. Everybody has on brand new clothes, shoes, coats. All the girls have new hairdos. And a few hair-don'ts. I found my locker, my brand new junior high school locker. I guess I was feeling cheesily happy.

And then what happened? Why upon starting the school year I immediately got hit with first-period Algebra. *Algebra*. On the first day of school. I thought it wasn't until later. That's what I get for not paying attention to my wonderfully printed schedule. Also, is it just me or is "algebra" a seriously funny sounding word? It's like the math gods warn you by their weird naming system that this thing you have to study is gonna be a curse.

I know there's *something* janky about algebra class, because about twenty minutes in, there was this incident. Roosh Punja dropped every single paper in his folder in front of his desk. All of his homework got mixed up. He had to sit there on the floor in front of everybody and straighten it out so he could find his algebra notes. Hmmmm. Roosh is like, the unclumsiest person I know. So I don't get why that happened. New school year nerves? Still...I laughed like everybody else. Then he gave me this look that made me feel like microwaved crap. I shouldn't have laughed at him. #JerkFaceMe. I also might be being overly spooky and totally connecting two things that are SO not connected. So maybe his accident was just rando and I'm reading too much into things as always.

So, Baron Winters and the Curse of Algebra. Oh, last year everyone kept saying 'Baron you can do it' and 'Baron you need to take this.' I got acquainted with fractions, decimals, and percentages and the only thing I could think was, 'why?' I understood the work but not the *point*. Seeing as how we all have calculators on our phones. And Ms. Bellicor is one of these teachers that just gets way too excited about their subject.

And in case we weren't having enough fun yet there's also Geometry coming up. Which comes right after the Algebra unit. It's like all the useless stuff lined right up in a row. So yeah we have to study cylinders, polygons and perpendicular lines. Um. Right so, unless I'm building a pyramid sometime soon I again must be missing the point. But it's necessary for the test that's (probably) going to change my life. So I just have to deal. I think I feel another invention coming on, but I'm not sure what it would be. How about Math Repellent?

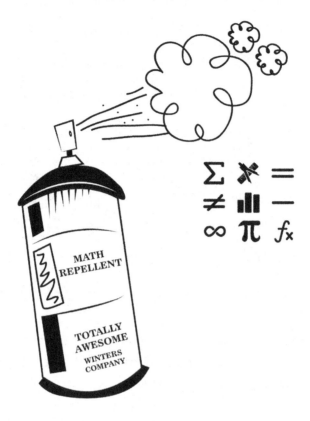

So of course after the first day, they figured out I need to be in Advanced Placement Math. Sure I do. But. Maybe it's a good thing. Maybe it can keep me away from Derek Kilroy.

CHAPTER 6

My dad told me I thought I was white.

Friday

I was so happy after that first round of testing because I had gotten 110%! Aced the work *and* the extra credit (without a calculator, natch) and it was my weekend to see my dad...wait am I writing a run-on sentence? Anyway so I showed dad my test scores and he just grunted. Then he said: "You think you a white boy or something, don't you?"

I...I didn't know what to say. I can't even talk to Chen about this one. Was I wrong for doing well on my test? Isn't that the point of school? I had been so excited before and my father's words made me feel like a balloon after a Tyrannosaurus-sized needle had been stuck into it. I wish there was a class at school called 'How to Become More Black.' Maybe then dad would be happier with me. I mean, I think he loves me...just maybe I'm not always the son he had in mind. Maybe.

CHAPTER 7

My teachers love me... so that means that the kids hate me.

Monday

Do you know the worst thing that could *ever* happen to a kid? That would be when your teacher stands you up in class and says publicly that you did an outstanding job. Last year in fifth grade, it was Raymie Nakagawa. She solved every math problem at lightning speed. And oh how the other kids just turned on her. I mean, like rabid dogs.

So guess who got the dreaded Teacher's Pet Crown of Shame today? Oh my lord WHY did Mr. McHale do THAT? So we were in third-period science, biology of all subjects. Right, I should know how a frog works but no classes on how *my* body works. Okay then. Well, all I did was follow his instructions to light the Bunsen burner and melt the wax in the crucible. I guess I did it faster than everybody else and now I don't want to go to lunch.

When I sat down? It was a CHORUS of death glares. Derek Kilroy was there. Of course, he was. My personal evil arch villain. Why do they call them 'arch?' Isn't that like how your heel surfs up to your toes? Anyway. Mr. McHale just went ON and ON about what a good job I had done like I had invented Infinite Bubble Gum™ or something. I almost threw my immaculately lit burner at the teacher just to get in trouble so he would stop complimenting me. But then I figured that trying to get into UnStare World? Yeah, trouble was pretty much not the way. As a side note, I'm just imagining inventing some actual Infinite Bubble Gum™.

You'd only need like one piece per chew because the sugar would never run out! Hey wait would that be bad for business?

Anyways Chen was there watching the whole thing. He understood how having the whole class glare at you turns your skin prickly like a Targtonian heat vision attack. He just doesn't seem to let it bother him when he gets complimented by Mr. HcHale. He's almost always the first one done with science experiments. He doesn't seem to care about who likes him or not. I need to learn something from Chen, I think.

It seems that being smart and Asian doesn't come with a daily butt whooping as an added feature. I wonder if there's a way to transfer coolth? Or maybe I could invent atransmo-ethnic ray and turn myself Asian. HAH. I'd love to see the look on mom's face when I got home THAT day. Oh well. At least the Spring Concert is still far away.

CHAPTER 8

Losing my virginity. iPass.

Wednesday

I swear upon all that is chocolate that if any assorted parental units or siblings happen to read this I will disavow all knowledge of its contents and BURN THE ENTIRE HOUSE DOWN. (And this means *you*, Christina. Dear. sister.) For the life of me I can't understand why everybody around me keeps talking about 'doing it.' I don't want to talk about 'doing it.' I'm not ready to 'do it.' I'm sure all the eighth graders are 'doing it' and bragging about it.

There seems to be this thing, this obsession, and it's like, all that people talk about. I just don't get it. Maybe my growth spurt is malfunctioning. Also, why do people talk about 'losing' their virginity?

Like, you were grabbing a slice of pizza and oops oh no I lost my gin gin at the restaurant? I bet Batman doesn't have days like this. So I'm not sure what I'm supposed to do until the hormones kick in. Judging by my siblings it seems like acne runs in this family. In the meantime maybe I'll try not to turn seventy-eight shades of red next time I'm in Phys Ed. Because for all the guys that are bathing in that wretched pubescent hormone shower? We are the Legion of Awkward.

CHAPTER 9

Phys Ed is where adults can legally humiliate us.

Friday

And speaking of gym class, why is this class even legal?

Maybe the teachers haven't noticed, but our bodies are YEAH LIKE HAYWIRE. It's no fun being an Almost Man. Yet another comment that, if spoken aloud, would probably get me principal office'd. Chen always seems unbothered, so he's like cool under pressure but Renee Garcia got so embarrassed today because. Well. Let's just say she's a woman now. Or something. I'm just sayin'. I'm not supposed to know these things! Or am I? I was never really invested in the concept of 'cooties' or anything. It's just more like girls are really different and no one is explaining what's going on.

Phys Ed teachers have the power to make us play sports we can't play. Great. So we (me and Chen) were playing basketball, or rather attempting to. That's another black person fail on my part, I can't shoot hoops worth kiffy. At least Chen doesn't laugh at me. So, of course, we started talking about girls. Chen has a funny attitude because he said that his parents will only allow him to date other Chinese girls. When he gets old enough that is. What's up with that? So of course right after Phys Ed Chen asks me, "Baron, what kind of girls do *you* like?" And I was like, "Ummm...the soft kind?" Do I have to pick a flavor? Is this multiple choice?

CHAPTER 10

Ch-yeah! Three day holiday weekend!

Monday

Columbus Day! For. The. Win. Me and Chen immediately texted each other when we woke up and said "Minecraft." I rode my bike to Chen's house like, right after I got out of bed. Of course I showered. Maybe. Cal Gordon and Billy Chertkow are coming over his house later but until then, it's me and Chen. I take screenshots and make them my phone wallpaper because why not? I'd always rather play on the computer because DUH max biomes and Chen seems better on his phone than I am. He does this really cool trick with customizing his skin too and makes some stuff fluorescent. We seriously need a new house Seed though. Like for reals. Some girls (like that stupid Lee Bell) brought some spawn eggs to school for a project because they wanted to make them 'pretty.' SPAWN EGGS AREN'T SUPPOSED TO BE PRETTY, FEMALES.

Whatever.

We're having too much fun for me to care. I was also told by my parentals that whenever I'm at Chen's house I'm not supposed to drink all the lemonade. Then when I'm there his mother is all like, "No, really, please drink all you want." I'm going to create a Minecraft mod called 'Mixed Messages' and dump all the adults I know into it because reasons. Explaining video games to my mom.

Monday Night

Know that feeling when you have to go home but don't want to? Yeah, that's like the Kids National Anthem. Mom asked me why I love to stay over at Chen's house. I try to explain the awesomeness that is Minecraft. But. I don't understand why I haven't learned my lesson about this. In most other things I'm not really a slow learner. Christina and Ezekiel tried to warn me; older sibling wisdom I guess. But it's like mom doesn't get it. I even showed her some parent forums online, and she keeps telling me that she's 'not into that online stuff' and she 'doesn't understand why your are either.' And then? She launches into this thing adults do, called 'When-I-was-Your-Age.'

Seriously that should be the name of a reality show where adults talk kids into tears. I'm not kidding. Plus. Mom. When you were my age you were a *girl*, so I doubt our lives have a lot of common experiences going on. Secondly, when you were my age phones were these big ugly things and then later you had "beepers." Just the name itself is mountains of LAME. So I just plaster my 'please don't smack me' smile on and keep listening. Why doesn't she talk to me about stuff that I actually need help on? Like that fact of how much I do not like Elisabeth Blue. Also. I do not like Elisabeth Blue. I *don't*.

CHAPTER 11

Why do I turn into an idiot when I talk to girls?

Elisabeth Blue

Okay. Maybe I *do* like Elisabeth Blue. Something strange happens when she walks into the room during second period. I just feel like my stomach's on vomit mode overload and then I turn red. Which is really funny looking when you have brown skin. I keep trying to fire up the courage to just go say 'hi,' buuuut...she has this stupid smirk on her face when she looks at me. And that stupid smirky look on her face? Makes me feel like I ordered a Stupid Burger with extra Stupid Cheese and some Diet Stupid to drink. Like she knows I like her or something and she's laughing because it'll never happen.

'It' meaning her being my girlfriend. Or something. I'm pretty sure that she likes Jimmy McClaren tho, and he's like four years taller than I am and is probably already shaving. Plus he's what they call a 'bad boy.' He's really rebellious and only half goes to class and smokes in the bathroom. So girls really dig that. I can see that life is going to be confusing.

Chen tried to talk to Elisabeth Blue a couple of times, but she just ignores him, with that same annoying smirk on her face. I don't know what's going on. I wish I could talk to my dad a little more honestly about these things. I also wish I could invent a Girl Translator™. That would completely solve my problems.

WHEN GIRLS SAY:
"NOTHING."
"I HATE YOU!"
"LEAVE ME ALONE."

THEY MEAN:
"EVERYTHING."
"I LOVE YOU."
"OH GOD PLEASE
TALK TO ME."

TOTALLY AWESOME
GIRL TRANSLATOR TM

WINTERS COMPANY

Can you imagine the money I could make and the FAME I could ACHIEVE with my Patented Girl Translator?? I'd be on every grown-up morning talk show in the nation. I could also sell my translator to every other boy in the sixth grade and make a fortune. I mean like, every sixth-grade boy in the *world*. Except for Jimmy McClaren because he obviously doesn't need one because my girlfriend clearly likes him. Except she's not really my girlfriend. It's possible I spend too much time thinking about Elisabeth Blue. It's a good thing I don't like her. Because I don't.

CHAPTER 12

The Vomit Monument.

Wednesday

I have to pass The Vomit Monument every Wednesday when I come out of English. There's this corner right as you turn from Purple Hall into Main Hall where the legendary Todd Jenkins threw up four years ago. He's obviously in high school now but his name is still known here. He's a legend because he hurled his breakfast and his lunch and probably his father's lunch that day; it's said he threw up for hours.

So much so until the janitors didn't even want to clean it up. So now, there's like this spot…and if you look close enough you can see the outline of his Puke Power[3] vomit fest. Nobody walks on it. I mean, *nobody.*

If you walk on it they say that a curse comes on you and you'll be the next one to throw up everything you ever ate at the worst possible time. Chen says he doesn't believe in superstitious stuff. I don't either. I think. I just know that with my luck I'll inherit a vomit monster curse and it'll wait until I get the courage to say 'hi' to Elisabeth Blue and then KER-SPLOOSHA-GURGLE. Even the Cool Girls, when they strut down Purple Hall (and WOW do they strut) completely avoid that spot. But us boys? We know It's the greatest monument of all time.

I think by the time I'm an old man the Mayor will have built a monument over it. *Monument Vomit,* by Todd Jenkins.

CHAPTER 13

"Oh, you've got *good* hair."

Thursday

Okay, so the Eighth Grade Queen of the Cool Girls, Sasha Peterson, every time she walks by me (as she did twice today but it's not like I'm counting) she rubs my hair. I don't get why, but she says it's 'good' hair. This has made many black kids hate me. My mother is black but she's also half Cherokee Indian and so she's got this really long, silky black hair. Mine is kind of curly but it's soft like hers. But I always get it cut really close to my head. Because. Maybe I'm trying to minimize the 'good hair' comments. But somehow Sasha still sees my hidden curliness and comments on it anyway. Such is my life. I've never really worn what they call "black" hairstyles. That fact seems to be (another) huge source of ire in the never-ending symphony of 'Reasons to Hate Baron.' Conducted by Le Idiot Extraordinaire Derek Kilroy.

It's one of the reasons Chen is my best bud; he never seems to trip on things like that. It's also things like that that make me tired of going to school, and I don't think I'm supposed to be tired of school at this age. So is "bad" hair the "regular black kind?" Is that like standard issue hair for black people or something? I don't really know if I've ever seen any of Chen's Chinese friends talk about his hair...as if somehow a different texture would make him "not really Chinese enough." Yeah, this kind of stuff fills up my little boy head with big boy headaches. Except I don't talk like that anymore because I'm all sixth gradey n' thangs. And no Spring Concert. Not yet anyway.

CHAPTER 14

Learning my Second-second language.

Friday

Right after lunch, I went to Blue Hall. It was time for the mandatory weekly meeting with the Guidance Counselor. First-floor office by the English classrooms. I was like, "I'm ready to receive guidance! Guide me! I'm student Guidey Guiderson up in here!" Okay, maybe I didn't actually say all that. Her office always smelled funny. Like…bleach and oranges. I can't possibly begin to imagine what was up with that. So I did the kid thing: pretended I didn't notice and smiled.

So according to Guide-ana, Queen of Bleached Oranges we have to take a language elective. Like English isn't enough with 'through,' 'though,' and 'thorough.' Everybody just uses text speak anyway so it's not like social media gives out grammar awards. Our choices are Spanish, French, and Russian. I guess I'll take Spanish. Not because I particularly like it, but speaking in French all the time sounds like a froo froo frog got stuck in your throat or something. And hearing Russian just makes me laugh. Another thing we're like never supposed to do, laugh at things that are funny. Are Russians funny?

Languages I think are cool. And I'm kind of learning another one on the side. Like, outside of school. Does that make me a spy? Anyway. It all happened when I met a man named Dr. Weppler at the Senior Center. I'll get to the Senior Center visit in a minute. Because like, a *lot* happened because of it. But in terms of languages, my time at the Senior Center had an added benefit. I met a really kind friend who took a liking to me. He was retired, but when he was working, he was a college professor. He also was a Protestant pastor, and he spoke five languages fluently. So mister Dr. Gregory Weppler began to teach me, of all things, Hebrew.

Teit	Cheit	Zayin	Vav	Hei	Dalet	Gimel	Beit	Alef
(T)	(Ch)	(Z)	(V/O/U)	(H)	(D)	(G)	(B/V)	(Silent)

Samekh	Nun	Nun	Mem	Mem	Lamed	Khaf	Kaf	Yod
(S)	(N)	(N)	(M)	(M)	(L)	(Kh)	(K/Kh)	(Y)

Tav	Shin	Reish	Qof	Tzadei	Tzadei	Fe	Pei	Ayin
(T/S)	(Sh/S)	(R)	(Q)	(Tz)	(Tz)	(F)	(P/F)	(Silent)

Wrote that out after two weeks. My chest was burst-ey with pride. The good kind of pride (I hope)! His caregiver actually started bringing Dr. Weppler to my mom's house once a week. Mom didn't mind, she seemed happy that I was learning.

Maybe I have a future in...I dunno. Maybe teaching? Or writing? I def love to do that. Maybe I could be an inventor! I'm kind of assuming that takes a lot of money tho. I don't see how it wouldn't. I certainly don't see myself as a pastor. Is that being selfish? I don't know. I always thought religious leader types weren't supposed to be thinking about girls. What do I know? I'm a kid. But if thinking about girls is a sin I'm on the express train to Hell with a first class seat.

CHAPTER 15

Of course, me and my best friend read comics.

Saturday

So it's possible, I'm not saying that it's true, but it's possible that I keep some of my comics at Chen's house so mom won't know how much allowance money I've spent on them. And I won't get started on my acid-free plastic storage bags or my extra width cardboard storage boxes for keeping my comics in perfect condition. Because geeks that's why.

I've also noticed that most black superheroes have the word 'black' in their names. At least they used to. Black Panther, Black Goliath, Black Lightning, although they went in a different direction with Storm and Vixen. I also like Batwing I. I think that Kaldur'ahm, or Aqualad, or 'Blackqualad' as we like to call him is my favorite. He has all the powers of Aquaman, he's young, strong, black and he's a leader. Earth-Two Superman is also black now.

I wonder if Chen thinks about these things? I don't think he does. We've never really talked about it at length. I need to ask him. I have to wonder if there's a thing with Asian based superheroes being his favorites or not. And SPEAKING of CONS, yes, I will find a way to go to San Diego Comic Con someday. Even if it kills me. Hoping for the non-lethal version of that tho. C2E2 here in Chicago is like my second home. I love it – love it – love it – love it – love it. Did I mention that I love it? Zeke takes me every year. This gives him mondo massive Cool Big Brother points. Also. I wonder if a certain someone who starts with Elisabeth and ends with Blue would ever do cosplay. She'd make an outstanding Mary Marvel. Not that I think about such things. Because I don't.

CHAPTER 16

So I won this Citizenship Award. Cool.

Tuesday

I got called to the office. My mind was a-racin' 'bout what for. But it wasn't about what I thought it was about. What it was actually about all started at the beginning of last summer. Me and several other kids in my class had been going to Camp Kacheekomi for two summers in a row. And it was mondo awesome. So it was my third summer there and I just loved it the way fish love water. Going to that camp was a kid's dream. I guess that's what summer day camps are for tho! (Also to give parents a break because apparently, our unlimited kid energy makes them take Grown-Up Crazy Bars.) Anyway. All day long at camp, it was softball, Frisbee, beaches, arts and crafts, archery, Capture the Flag. You name it. Even Ice Cream Fridays. That's it! I'm becoming a Camp Director when I grow up. Where's the downside?

So it was like the fourth week of camp. Things had been going awesomely. And routinely. But after four weeks of regular regularness, we got to camp grounds one day and they said not to get off the bus. At first, we were confused, but then we figured it out. Surprise field trip! We were like, SCORE! Who doesn't love surprise field trips? Except for the ones where you get gum in your hair. Those are Lord Anti-Fun invasions. So anyway we were off into our totally unannounced field trip. I was hoping that food was going to be involved at our surprisey destination. Holy hot wings it was a really long bus ride. We had to go on the highway and everything. Finally, we got to where we were going: the Senior Center.

The center was this really tall orange-ish building on the far west side of town. Of course, we passed all the fast food places right before we got there and I realized that kids can't ignore the smell of French fries. I think also that I need to invent fast food peanut butter sandwiches because like NOBODY has them. At any rate, they unloaded us off the bus (which took a minute) and gathered all us kids with our counselors in the front lobby. Then they said they wanted a few kids to volunteer to read stories with some of the residents. My hand shot up before I knew it. Turned out that reading with the seniors was really, really fun. Most of the seniors that I talked to had some awesomely funny stories to tell. Very few of them were black. I noticed that right away. I didn't really care tho, and neither did they. More than one of the ladies said that I reminded them of their grandson. That made me feel really warm inside. In an 'aw shucks' kind of way. Yep, I think I was black kid blushing because I felt the prickly skin a-pricklin'. We stayed all day, and I made some new senior friends. It was the bomb.

So that totally sweet visit to the Senior Center is what led to a bunch of us Kacheekomi campers getting called to the office during sixth period. 'Ceptin' we didn't know that on the way there. That's like the most unwanted thing that can happen to a kid besides the Teacher's Pet Crown, the Purpose-Obscured Main Office visit. Holy cow my knees shook so hard I thought they were breaking up with my legs. We all looked at each other as we were walking with the bug eyes you get when you think your life is about to be over. We got to the main office and the secretary told us to sit down on the bench right outside the principal's office. Yeah at the same time I felt my pee coming I was thinking, "my parents are gonna kill me." Pupil to Principal's Office to Parents is the dreaded Three P circus and no thank you. Principal Pratt opened his office door...and there was a big smile on his face.

Know that feeling where your pee is coming and then your brain tells it to change its mind? Principal Pratt told us we were getting a Citizenship Award for spending time with the residents at the Senior Center last summer. Lexi, the camp counselor that chaperoned us, obviously wasn't there. I thought she should have been. I thought that maybe she should get the credit. Principal Pratt said they were giving us kids the award. And I was like, wow. I felt so proud, I'm sure I was beaming.

Thursday

So Thursday that week there was an official assembly and Principal Pratt called all of us camp kids who had read with the seniors to the stage. He called us one by one for extra spotlighting. Then he handed us a *Certificate of Good*

Citizenship and I think I smiled so hard my teeth wanted to pay my mouth extra rent.

CHAPTER 17

Aaaaand then Derek beat the crap out of me.

So of course, whenever anything good happens in my life, I think it sends out Bully C'mere vibes. Guess who was waiting for me outside right after my moment of Citizenship Awardiness? That's right, Derek Kilroy, a boy who had taken a particular liking to kicking me in the whoopsidaisy. Repeatedly. He followed me back to my locker and then the other kids turned down Green Hall. Holy blueberries I tried to run. I mean, I did run but it didn't do any good. I ran outside and got as far as the soccer fields before he tripped me. I hit the ground really hard. And Killer Kilroy started beating me until I thought my ribs had turned into macaroni.

He said if I screamed for help he'd find me after school and we'd go for Round Two. So I lamely tried to defend myself and he just laughed and kept rearranging my face. I'd survived before so I figured I'd survive this time. It's not like the nonexistent school security guards were around or anything. Oh no, they saved their appearances for when we were dropping candy wrappers on the running track or wearing the wrong t-shirt.

CHAPTER 18

What kind of a name is 'Baron,' anyway?

Thanksgiving Break

The holiday was as good a time as any to let my face heal from being lumpy and purple. The nationally sanctioned oinkfest on Thursday helped take my mind off of school. When I get into fights my mom is like, useless. She keeps saying that she'll come to the school and talk to Principal Pratt. And the Gang of Bullies. Right. I'm like, doesn't she get that THEE LAST THING a boy needs is his mother coming to the school for him? I would never live that down if I lived to be older than Yoda. Sometimes I fight. No seriously I really do. It's just that those guys are eighth graders and they're stronger and faster. Sometimes if I fight back they make it last longer. If I take a good punch or two and I'm bent over from the pain, they move on. Sometimes. I wish my dad had taught me freaking kung-fu or something.

Speaking of my dad, I keep meaning to ask him why he named me 'Baron.' He's never told me, although I suspect it's a riff on my grandfather's name, 'Byron.' I also love those long holiday times with him. I wonder how much my dad saw his dad? Is that like a pattern? He asked me what had happened to my face. I didn't say anything because I knew how he'd react. I'd win the Wuss-of-all-Wusses Crown again, at least in his eyes. So I just told him I fell off my skateboard. I felt like if he wasn't going to teach me how to fight he had no right to laugh at me for not knowing how. But thoughts like that, if spoken aloud, get you sent to your room with jumbo size slappage marks all upside your head. I'd had enough of being walloped for one week. And by 'week' I mean 'lifetime.' Oh well, I'd still have fun with the Dadster. Movies hooooooooo!

That Thanksgiving meal, mom really put her heart and soul into that. Did I mention my parents have a strange relationship? Anyway. Dad and I, after that serious belly buster of a food fest, watched TV. He always liked shark movies, because they made him laugh. He would constantly comment on how stupid the people in them were. I think my fave quote of his was, "These fools need to stay out the water! Because Boy, I ain't ever seen a shark crawl up on dry land and eat nobody!" Hahaha that always cracked me up. Because it was so true. Maybe I get my penchant for smart mouth truth from the Dadster.

Maybe my life was a shark movie and Derek Kilroy was a great white.

CHAPTER 19

Ouch. I thought shaving would be cool.

Saturday

I have, like negative stubble. My voice still sounds like I'm Peter Pan with a serious suntan. Dad had stayed over and fallen asleep on that old brown couch in the TV room. Mom just will not throw that dusty couch away. So he's snoring and I'm awake bright and early. So for some bizarre reason, I asked Ezekiel if I could watch him shave. And by 'watch' I meant 'try and shave myself.' It seems that you actually have to have facial hair for that to make sense, and my big brother just laughed at me for cutting myself. I have to admit I thought it was pretty funny too.

Maybe I'm still trying to rush this puberty thing. I filled the sink with hot water, and put some shaving cream on my face (and ooooh whatever menthol is it has to be illegal for little kids to use it because it smells so good). I brought the razor up to my cheek and with one scrape I thought I was gonna tear off the side of my head. Or maybe bleed to death. That would've been easier. Ezekiel meanwhile is laughing his head off. I needed a paramedic and my brother was laughing while I died. Anyway. Turns out that shaving requires...what was that word Ezekiel used? Oh yeah, 'finesse.' He said talking to girls does too but that's another thing. Maybe I should wait until my non-stubble turns into actual hair. Adventures in almost puberty. Maybe I'll just grow a manly man beard and never shave! Baron Beardo! Okay, holy cow that's a villain name from like black and white movies but okay.

CHAPTER 20

No... my diet is actually NOT an indicator of my intelligence.

DECEMBER

Monday

It hasn't snowed yet, but it will. I look forward to it. That's part one of the countdown right after Thanksgiving, the days until the first real heavy snow. That's the best part about growing up in Chicago. Real white Christmases. When I talk to some of my cousins out west they tell me about how they have no snow and no real pizza. I can't imagine life without either. Give me the Midwest any day.

So I hop on the bus to school that morning. We were all counting down to Christmas break because that's the second big countdown after Turksgiving. A bunch of us in the middle of the bus were yammering about different things. Mainly our assorted opinions on family members. And the laughability of the PG-13 rating idea. Do parents really think we have limited access to content? I'd like to introduce them to the internet. It's a thing. Then somehow we got to talking about what our Thanksgiving meals consisted of. Derek Kilroy, one of the banes of my existence, said "Of course you had fried chicken. That's what *you people* eat."

Ummm...I didn't get that. Nor why he felt the need to comment at all, but then again...every interaction with him was a precursor to the next fight. He said it like eating fried chicken (which we rarely ate anyway) made me stupider than him or something. If Chen ate fried chicken, would he be stupid? Anyway, fried chicken is good. Strawberries are good. Lemon cake is REALLY good, and people are stupid. People like Derek anyway. Every time I think this idiot can't irritate me anymore he wins a new Crown in Kingdom Vexation.

CHAPTER 21

Cutting farts pretty much define your social life.

Tuesday

About a week after that lovely chicken conversation, we were getting off the bus to go to first period class. And Aiden Easton, one of the best Mathletes in the state, committed the cardinalest sin ever. Aiden cut the cheese. Ripped a corker. Dropped a bomb. Right in the front of the bus. All loud and unmistakably him. And we all roared with laughter. We roared until the bus driver shouted and told us to calm down. After that, Aiden got his new name from a bunch of girls in second period, they called him the Fartlete. I thought that was pretty funny. Aiden was blush faced about it all day, so maybe not so funny to him. That's going to be his name from now on though, no question. If I had a genie, my three wishes would be:

1. Don't let me fart in public.

2. Break Derek Kilroy's face.

3. *Please* don't let me fart in public.

CHAPTER 22

Lunchtime AKA The Cafeteria is the Bane of My Existence.

Wednesday

If Hell had a portal to Earth it would be the school cafeteria. Why? Because the cafeteria is the place where you have to draw all your Friend District lines. Like, are the people who hung with me in 5th grade still going to be my friends now? Do I have to sit with the smart kids? Do I have to sit with the geek kids? Are smart kids geeks? Are geek kids smart? And the big kahuna of questions, can I go back to either group after having been seen with the other? And which group qualifies me as "black enough?" Fortunately, Chen was right there. But I spent the whole lunch period wondering, what was going to happen on those days when he wasn't? Or wanted to sit with some other friends?

The cafeteria is where all clique eggs come to be hatched. Period. The teachers treat the black kids differently but we have to act like they don't. Derek Kilroy (who is an enemy so I don't even know why I consider anything he says) stated that the teachers thought that I was "one of the *good* ones." What the heck does *that* mean? I don't think I'm supposed to be this stressed at eleven years old. I really don't. The lunch that mom had packed was delicious as usual; a corned beef sandwich with mayo & mustard, apple slices, blue corn tortilla chips, celery sticks, and a juice box. Chen for some reason wanted to trade his chocolate peanut butter bar for my celery sticks and I was like 'heck yeahs' and then it was *nom nom nom nom.*

Friday

And then the sweetest sound known to children all over the world...the bell announcing Winter Break! Seriously, is there a better sound in life? If there is, I've never heard it!

CHAPTER 23

Ho ho ho.

Christmas Week

School's out, I'm home, mom lets me have all the chocolate I want. SCORE! I think this is always the happiest time all year. I mean, my brother and sister actually sit still long enough to interact with the family! Mom cooks up a storm, dad's generally in a good mood (although sometimes I'm pretty sure he's been drinking! *snicker*). All my aunts come over, from both sides, and my mother is the hostess. My aunts all have really different personalities. And they're all really light skinned. Mom's the darkest one, I'm sure that's a thing with them. Anyway, personality-wise, my aunts: one is really friendly, another is really private, one has been married to my uncle for a long time, and one has a different boyfriend every time we see her. But they've got one thing in common: they all sure can cook. I've got this one aunt, Aunt Jennifer, who cooks, like, all the desserts from every cookbook. No seriously.

She brings lemon cake, and sweet potato pies. And apple cobbler. And fruit-filled Jell-O. Sometimes I wonder why she's not a professional chef. We eat until all stomach lining is crying for mercy. We don't always get presents every year but when we do, dad goes all out. I mean, I'm still loving my bike from last year and he bought my sister this pendant she's been wanting for a while.

They were both so happy. Mom is not really a gift receiver, although she gives us plenty of stuff, usually clothes. It seems to make her happy just to be with the fam. But with her sisters flying in, that sets the stage for...

CHAPTER 24

Attack of the Cousins

Saturday

When my aunts bring all my cousins with them, that's always buckets of fun. Except for this one cousin. More on her in a minute. My aunts are all musical. They will strike up all these Christmas songs and then perfectly harmonize with one another. Like they're the whole worship team at their church back home, seriously. They should be their own girl group.

I often wonder if I could learn an instrument...like, I bet they're fun to play once you get the hang of them. But UGH, that everyday practice thing would *not* be my friend.

So I've got this one cousin, Qmella, who seems to have a perpetual zit farm on her face. Me and my other cousins here call her 'Queen of Pus' because the number of blackheads she must've popped have to number in the thousands. Plus she's got a great big ugly smile full of cavities and Hell. And by Hell I mean, she's one of those people who is low-key evil. She's super nice in front of the adults and kind of has them fooled. But when it's just us kids and the grownups aren't around? Holy cow she talks about us like we're the human equivalent of gum stuck in a water fountain. Yeah it's not pretty.

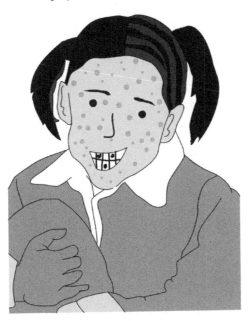

So anyway, evil cousins aside, after a while the adults always get tired of that patent pending Endless Kid Energy for Jumping on Stuff and send us away. Either to the basement to play or outside, they don't much care where. Even in winter. I don't have enough controllers for us all to play video games at the same time anyway, so we normally do Frisbee Football in the snow if there is any. Which is mega mondo fun. The girls are always convinced that they can beat us. They can't, but it's a good effort. Geez, I sound like a coach from school.

CHAPTER 25

It's Tradition.

So...y'know how most families have like, normal fun things they do at the holidays? Well, my dad and my Uncle Marques fired up their most favorite tradition: The After Dinner Farting Contest. Oh lord help me, Jesus. My father just leaned over and ripped a fart so loud the people on TV heard it. And then my uncle started smiling and let loose a whopper that felt like an earthquake got lost on its way to Albania. And then...my father unleashed the scariest weapon that a behind can generate: a silent but deadly nuke. I mean it smelled so bad he cleared the room in less than thirty seconds, which has to be a new record or something. My mother didn't say anything, she just went and got the fan and kept it moving. I hope with all of my eleven-year-old heart that I'm not looking at my future. Otherwise just shoot me now.

CHAPTER 26

Fire up the Converters

JANUARY

New Year's Week

(For the record, every time I hear Luke say "fire up the converters" to Artoo I get this major geek rush. Like seriously my head feels woozy. Dad likes the old *Star Wars* movies the best. He says they're the originals. I'm always like, isn't the first *Star Wars* movie you see the original one for *you?* Yeah, sometimes I overthink things. I think.) ANYWAY It's time for a New Year, and we always go to church on New Year's Eve. We stay there past midnight, normally all the way to 6 am or so on New Year's Day. More singing, holding hands and ringing in the new year, but in the totally religious way. Like, without alcohol. Not that I know anything about that. My personal favorite part is when the service is over and there's that fresh smell of bacon and pancakes coming from the basement kitchen. They really shouldn't allow those smells to waft up to the sanctuary while we're praying because who can (no offense God) keep thinking about holiness and heavenly things when that smell is dancing all up in your nose? The rest of New Year's week is almost always the same...the most enjoyable sleep of my life, and me and Chen playing Minecraft until our noses bleed. Yes that has happened.

CHAPTER 27

Starting my career as a writer.

It's almost time to go back to school, and I normally get kind of writey along through here. Writing thoughts in a notebook is not really news to me, because...back when I was a kid (last year) I wrote a book that people seemed to love called, *Grumpy, Lumpy, Frumpy and Stumpy, A Farty Boys Tale.*

- *87* -

I won several creative awards at school (because I drew all of the pictures too), and I even won a *Promising Young Writer Award* from the Regional Writers Guild. I was so happy and proud, and all because I wrote about four brothers having a fart adventure. (And their ONE awful cousin. I'm not looking at YOU Qmella. Okay, maybe I am.) My dad asked me why the people in the book were all white. I didn't say anything and just looked at my mom. She smiled because she got it. I wanted to tell dad that they were white because maybe I was low-key trying to act like I wasn't talking about my own family. DUHR.

Anyway. Sometimes the adults and assorted teachers are surprised at my writing skills. Maybe they think that as a kid I shouldn't be able to write like that. But I've always loved to write. And apparently, I'm good at it. I'm not going to be doing any of that 'when I grow up' kind of writing tho. Because. That's the kid equivalent of mom's 'When I was your age' lectures. Also. I'm in sixth grade. Which it's time to get back to.

CHAPTER 28

No boy should ever have to wear new shoes to school.

Monday

Going back to school always makes it seem like you didn't even have a break. Also, sometimes my school is so hot because the heat is on blast, we change into summer clothes while inside. No seriously. They don't seem to be able to make the heat work right. Speaking of things working right, let's get this one thing straight: the universe has decreed a divine cosmic jest. Said jest states that:

No girl that you like will EVER like you

and

Thee last girl on earth you'd ever notice

will think you're a rock star.

Um, yeah Audrey Plurry. I cannot stand her. And she watches every single thing I do. So as soon as I walked in school with my new shoes on, she announced it to the entire class. And for what reason I do not understand.

"Check out Baron Winters' new shoes. He thinks he's SO COOL!" I actually did not think I was cool. I thought I was in a winter month in a busted down school so janky that I had to wear summer clothes on the inside. Also. My new shoes were far too big. I didn't think I was anything but Captain Appledork. And oh lord she couldn't wait to put me on blast. My mother tells me that backwards girl logic (that was actually my phrasing) means that the more a girl likes you, the more she'll pick on you. Great. Just great. That must mean that Audrey is so in love with me she would marry me five times. The Reverse Gene is female and I'm just about done. Need that Girl Translator, brain. Need that translator.

CHAPTER 29

Yeah this is awful from every angle.

FEBRUARY

Tuesday

So, Valentine's Day is like a girl holiday. It's like the girliest girl holiday of all time. And so, of course, the geniuses at school figure we should continue to send candy hearts. Like we were still in third grade or something. Maybe they don't realize the pressure that comes along with this process. What if no one likes you? What if you get no hearts? What if you send hearts to someone and they hate you for it? I don't understand why adults rule the world. It was fifth period, we just got back from lunch. So of course, everything that I thought would happen, happened.

The cutest girls with the womanliest shapes got the mostest hearts. The jockiest jocks and the thuggiest thugs got the credit for all the anonymous ones. But that's just because the girls already liked them anyway. Because girls. Then there was like, everybody else. All turning redder than a sponge in an emergency room because no hearts? Yeah, that means you're totally not cool. A Losey Loserson. I also sometimes grab some of the leftover hearts and shove a bunch of them in my mouth before the teacher notices. Which often results in drool crunching and stomach pain later on.

So it would be nice if I didn't have the kind of mind that was wondering what Elisabeth Blue was thinking about me right now. Because I'm sure she isn't because I'm not Jimmy. Which is why this day is made of homemade distilled UGH but hey who's counting? At least it's not the Spring Concert.

CHAPTER 30

Daydreaming.

Thursday

I wonder why they call it "daydreaming?" Because it's obviously in the day, but you're not really dreaming. You have to be asleep to be dreaming, right? So I guess I'll call it "daythinking" which is what I guess I do most of the time. Sitting in first period homeroom, staring out of the window, I finished my classwork a while ago. Watching everybody run around outside playing, and....ooooh! Cross-country skiing! My favorite. I wonder if I could ever join that team. I'm not an athlete but maybe it's worth a shot. Then again I think about the endless questions from mom if I did ever attempt to play a sport.

But know what I think? I think that moms like to fuss over kids. Because I've noticed that no matter what you do, your mom will fuss. At least mine does. I hope I can try out for the skiing team when I get to high school. Assuming of course that I survive junior high school. And the test of all tests will answer that question definitively. I've seen TV shows about people who hit the lottery and like, their entire life is different. All that casharoni, they say, enables them to live their dreams. Well, maybe my hopefully impending test is like the lottery for kids. Hopefully. Then I had to snap out of my day thinking because the teacher was giving me the 'what are you doing' look. So back into pretend-to-do-homework-I've-already-finished mode.

CHAPTER 31

Hot Dog Hell.

MARCH

Friday

I'm convinced that some foods were invented by the devil. School hot dogs are one of them. No seriously. Know why? They taste so good when they're good. But too many of them and your stomach will hurt big time. But when they're bad? They're REALLY bad. For some reason, they serve us hot dogs almost every day during the month of March. Don't know why. I only eat them on Friday because that's the only day that mom doesn't pack me a lunch. She says the school needs to feed us sometimes because of tax dollars or something.

So anyway they give us these hot dogs but they're like.... I dunno not even brown sometimes. They're sometimes almost gray, YUCK. If you smother them with enough ketchup and mustard then you can't taste the blecch. But I'm like, could the school give us dogs like you get at a baseball game!!?? Those are like the best dogs ever. Or maybe like the Memorial Day cookout dogs, those are pretty good too. Guess the devil didn't invent those brands. Anyway. We were sitting at the Geek Table in the cafeteria and we all realized one thing: those ugly pieces of mystery meat make better weapons than they do food. So Chen stuck a hot dog down my back. So I naturally tried to stick one down his shirt. Then it was pretty much just a food fight. A fact which we quickly denied when the cafeteria monitor came over.

Oh LORD, we could've gotten into so much trouble if it hadn't been Mr. McComb on lunchroom duty. He's one of those hall monitor adults that actually seems to like kids. So he told us to break it up and clean up our mess and didn't write us up for it. Holy cow it was my lucky day. So me and Chen looked at each other with that "to be continued" look we have. Hah it was great. Also. If I had come home with a detention slip for food fighting in the cafeteria my mother would've slapped my nose to Baltimore. Because for some reason, I've discovered that if adults think you're smart but especially smart and black, you can't ever do anything wrong. And by "wrong" I mean "normal," like shoving hot dogs down your best friend's shirt. If I had known that "smart" equals "jail" I would've asked God to give me muscles instead.

CHAPTER 32

April belongs to Ollie.

APRIL

Wednesday

It's Springy spring time. The weather is breaking. So the only thing that's happening now is rehearsal, rehearsal, rehearsal. Mr. Picard is the Choir Director and Ms. Ollie is the Band Director and man do they make all the music kids work extra hard during the month of April. I guess it's because they need to prepare for the Godzilla of all junior high events, the Spring Concert (*shudder*). If you're just a casual regular student type dude like me, we only have to rehearse once per week. But it's like the music kids have no life outside of practice. Then again I guess learning to read notes is like learning a whole other language. Also, the band room is where the kids who smoke go to smoke. There's also a rumor that Mr. Picard smokes with them. But don't quote me on that.

CHAPTER 33

No one likes the month of Maying. – Spring Concert Part 1

MAY

Wednesday

So. It's almost here. I can barely contain my exciteyness. I'm talking about my test, not the Spring Concert. My older brother Zeke told me that singing in a school choir as a kid was a rite of passage. I was like, do kids get a vote in that?

All the teachers seem to really get their engines revved by the idea of the annual Spring Concert. Standing us kids up on risers wearing moronic black pants and lame white shirts. Add ugly black ties and making us sing songs that dead people sang four-umpteen-a-google years ago and you've got a bucket of fun. Don't they know that some boys have changing voices and the worst feeling in life is to think in complete sentences but when you speak your voice sounds like Attack of the Frog People??? When I read the words to these songs I think, no one talks that way anymore. But anyway, this Ultra Megadork Humiliation Fest is coming up in a few weeks and there's all this extra rehearsal after school. And all of the boys on the back riser seem to think that rehearsal means, "please burp loudly now."

CHAPTER 34

Please don't make me sing in front of people. – Spring Concert Part 2.

Friday

It's here. *The* day. Spuh-ring Concert. For some reason we can't just cancel class and sing, oh no, we have to come **back** to school. At least I have the comfort of knowing that I don't have a solo. Because every boy that sings a solo is candy apple red before he finishes because it's about the most lastest activity that could ever be wanted. In this life or any other. And I of course, standing at the roaring height of an elf am on the front row.

And then it happened.

The guy on my right, Calvin? He started peeing his pants, and it was dripping down his leg. He was so nervous he couldn't hold it. So now I have to stand up there and pretend that I don't smell that four-gallon pee parade that's happening right next to me. In between songs Mr. Picard tried to discreetly get some towels and then let him go to the bathroom, but how do you discreetly do all that? Then the girls next to him started giggling and before you know it we were ALL consumed with gigglage.

And then Mr. Picard gave us the ugliest look this side of the devil in an outhouse and we had to focus and keep singing. I told you this thing was rancid. Now Calvin will forever be "that kid that peed on stage during Spring Concert." Yeah, that's sure the way I'd want to be remembered, you betcha. Did I mention that there are no other black kids in the choir? I feel like I was chosen to be that black kid that does all the stuff that black kids don't do. Then if I say that out loud, somehow I'm accused of using hate speech or some other malarkey. So I can't talk about my life, because by stating facts, like, I'M THE ONLY BLACK KID IN THE CHOIR it makes me some kind of racist lunkhead. Okay then. I'll just stand here and be black. Casually. But I won't *look* like I'm standing here casually being black. Because racism.

CHAPTER 35

The Best News of My Life.

JUNE

Tuesday

So the Spring Concert is nothing but a memory and it's all Juneish now. And sure enough, I'm gearing up for summer. But there's one little piece of news I've been anticipating since last summer. Not like I've been counting the days or holding my breath okay SO DOING BOTH. So I'm standing in the kitchen with the fam while dad is on one of his paternal graced stopbys. They (my parents) are both smiling. Christina and Ezekiel seem unusually glowy too. So it feels like everybody's in Happy Land when they look at me. Um. I swear that's the most crazy-awkward feeling in the world (besides wearing gym shorts when your boy body decides to become a man body). And then my padre and my madre tell me the best news of my life.

In a nutshell, all lights are green for me to take the test. *The test.* The one that determines if I might be able to skip a grade. My mind went crazy with excitement! If I pass this thing, would I become the world's youngest eighth grader? DUHN DUHN DUHN!! Would I make new friends? Could I (gasp).... possibly even become one of the *Cool Kids??* Could I do the unthinkable and clique hop??? Do they even accept applications for Team Cool Kids if you've skipped a grade? Because if they do and I get in, that would have to score points with girls. Which would be Dude Nirvana because POINTS WITH GIRLS. So at test-time, I have to go to the same room that they give detention in on Saturday morning. And the test has, like, a *lot* of sections. Mom says I have to study and bought me some special test-taking books. I am strangely not nervous. Well. Maybe a little. I don't think I have butterflies in my stomach, more like a bass subwoofer cranked to eleven when it makes your teeth start to rattle. Could that fit in my stomach? Okay, my rambling is a clear sign that I'm not nervous.

YEAH UM.

SO. STINKING. NERVOUS.

Maybe I'll eat a nice gray hot dog. That always calms the nerves.

CHAPTER 36

The Moment of Truth.

Saturday

So I have this thing that I do before I take a really important test. I listen to Batman's theme song. No, not the one from a long time ago. The one from the animated series. It makes me feel like I can do anything. And I so totally can because Bruce Wayne is my hero and role model.

Mom drove me to school. She was humming the whole way. That's a sign that she's happy when she does that. And when she's happy I'm happy. So I was nervous happy. Happy nervous. We arrived and mom gave me a 'you can do it' kiss. I think that's a special mom superpower I kid you not.

I walked into the school and went to the study hall aka the Detention Room where the test was being given. I sat down. I dropped my pencils on the floor. Like five of them. People laughed. I think it was karma for me laughing at Roosh. I could be wrong. I quickly flipped through the pages of the test as soon as I got it. So much material. History, science, math, English. And I had to score in the 90th percentile to even be considered for the grade skipping. My hands might've started trembling, I'm not sure. But I didn't care. I was ready.

CHAPTER 37

The Test Scores Arrive.

Wednesday

Two weeks after that magic test taking Saturday, and I was learning how a caged tiger felt. I came to understand why they paced back and forth in their cages. Because that's all I was doing. Pacing. Back and forth. Every afternoon I'd keep going back and forth between my room and the kitchen. Then I'd open the refrigerator. You know, the way you do when you think maybe some new food has grown in there since the last time you opened it. I knew I was getting on mom's nerves. But I couldn't help it. I had taken *the* test. There were questions there from every single subject I had during the school year. Including music; wasn't expecting that. I missed it on my initial flip through. I still felt like I aced almost every section of the exam. But that could've just been me being overconfident. Then again if I were really confident I wouldn't have been pacing, now would I?

American History and I still weren't the best of friends. But either way, I felt like my life was(possibly) going to change forever. That feeling just would not leave me. The monitors at the test site said that it would take about two weeks for the results to arrive and that they would be mailed to my parents directly. I had kind of hoped they would give them to me in school. So I could deal with the moment of knowing on my own. And by myself first. That way, if there was any disappointment, I didn't have to show it in front of mom. Or my dad. I could brace myself for whatever the parental units were going to say. So I naturally of course began to count the SECONDS from the time I turned in my papers until precisely two weeks had elapsed. That Wednesday had brought the grand waiting time total up to two weeks and four days.

And then it happened.

The mail came. Because I, of course, had also been running to the window to watch the mailbox like a wolf watches its dinner. Our mailman's a really cool dude who always says 'Hey Baron' whenever he sees me. I wanted to buy him a pizza with all the toppings when I saw him bring the Envelope of the Immaculate Manila. I just knew it HAD to be my test scores.

Just had to be. Mom went out to get the mail and got a funny smile on her face. She walked back inside and said we'd open it and read it together. Not the scenario I had imagined. My lungs felt like they weighed four thousand pounds.

Mom opened the envelope and slowly (a snail would've been in warp seven compared to her) pulled out the test scores. She stared at them and then looked at me. She had a completely neutral look on her face.

I didn't look at them with her like she wanted. I snatched them out of her hand and ran up to my room. I slammed the door. I was pretty sure that would make her mad. But I did it anyway. She didn't follow me, so maybe she got the message. I might've been low-key crying a little bit but don't expect me to admit it because guy card. I was, however, trembling with questions.

Literally trembling. Should I have prepared better? Did I make the cut? What percentage did I get right or wrong? Would Elisabeth Blue *ever* be my girlfriend? (Okay wait maybe she was unrelated to the exam thing.) Anyway. It was time, time, TIME for me to look at them. The blessed test scores. Time to find out the one thing I had been waiting all year to know:

Was my life about to change?

About the Author

DAVID TAYLOR II

David Taylor II is an author, playwright, songwriter and producer. He writes sci fi, fantasy, comic books, and Children's Literature. He is the author of the new children's favorite, *Diary of a Chocolate Midas* and is also adding to his *Dear God* children's series.

His latest novel, *Lucifer: Soldiers, Serpents and Sin* is an internationally best-selling book. He has created an entire story world called *The Realm* from that first book and continues to expand it.

He is a co-composer for the smash hit theater production, *Eye of the Storm:The Bayard Rustin Musical,* nominated for 3 Black Theater Alliance awards.

In 2015 his book *Wayward Pines:Survival,* from the hit Fox TV show of the same name, broke top 10 in the Amazon best seller list and is currently still in the Top 100 of Kindle Worlds sci fi.

He is the proud father of two, as well as a lover of football, pizza, and a good glass of lemonade.

- Email: Books@DT2Author.org
- Twitter: @DT2Author
- Website: www.DT2Author.org

Made in the
USA
Monee, IL